Playing with Plays™ Presents Shakespeare's

Taming of the Shrew
FOR KIDS

(The melodramatic version!)

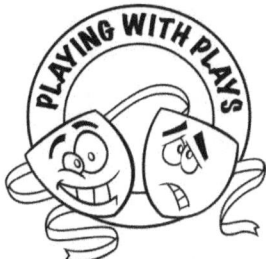

For 8-19+ actors, or kids of all ages who want to have fun!
Creatively modified by
Khara C. Barnhart and Brendan P. Kelso
Cover illustrated by Shana Hallmeyer
Cover Characters by Ron Leishman
Special Contributor: Asif Zamir

3 Melodramatic Modifications of Shakespeare's Play
for 3 different group sizes:

8-9 Actors

10-13 Actors

14-19+ Actors

Table Of Contents

For Mike
- KCB

KPK, never quit being witty with your words
- BPK

Playing with Plays™ – Shakespeare's Taming of the Shrew for Kids

Copyright © 2004-2024 by Brendan P. Kelso, Playing with Plays LLC
Some characters on the cover are ©Ron Leishman ToonClipart.com

For performance rights please see
page 6 of this book or contact:

contact@PlayingWithPlays.com

www.PlayingWithPlays.com

Printed in the United States of America
Published by Playing With Plays LLC

ISBN: 1470133679
ISBN: 978-1470133672

Foreword

When I was in high school there was something about Shakespeare that appealed to me. Not that I understood it mind you, but there were clear scenes and images that always stood out in my mind. Romeo & Juliet, "Romeo, Romeo; wherefore art thou Romeo?"; Julius Caesar, "Et tu Brute"; Macbeth, "Double, Double, toil and trouble"; Hamlet, "to be or not to be"; A Midsummer Night's Dream, all I remember about this was a wickedly cool fairy and something about a guy turning into a donkey that I thought was pretty funny. It was not until I started analyzing Shakespeare's plays as an actor that I realized one very important thing, I still didn't understand them. Seriously though, it's tough enough for adults, let alone kids. Then it hit me, why don't I make a version that kids could perform, but make it easy for them to understand with a splash of Shakespeare lingo mixed in? And voila! A melodramatic masterpiece was created! They are intended to be melodramatically fun!

THE PLAYS: There are 3 plays within this book, for three different group sizes. The reason: to allow educators or parents to get the story across to their children regardless of the size of their group. As you read through the plays, there are several lines that are highlighted. These are actual lines from the original book. I am a little more particular about the kids saying these lines verbatim. But the rest, well... have fun!

The entire purpose of this book is to instill the love of a classic story, as well as drama, into the kids.

And when you have children who have a passion for something, they will start to teach themselves, with or without school.

These plays are intended for pure fun. Please DO NOT have the kids learn these lines verbatim, that would be a complete waste of creativity. But do have them basically know their lines and improvise wherever they want as long as it pertains to telling the story. Because that is the goal of an actor: to tell the story. In A Midsummer Night's Dream, I once had a student playing Quince question me about one of her lines, "but in the actual story, didn't the Mechanicals state that 'they would hang us'?" I thought for a second and realized that she had read the story with her mom, and she was right. So I let her add the line she wanted and it added that much more fun, it made the play theirs. I have had kids throw water on the audience, run around the audience, sit in the audience, lose their pumpkin pants (size 30 around a size 15 doesn't work very well, but makes for some great humor!) and most importantly, die all over the stage. The kids love it.

One last note: if you want some educational resources, loved our plays, want to tell the world how much your kids loved performing Shakespeare, want to insult someone with our Shakespeare Insult Generator, or are just a fan of Shakespeare, then hop on our website and have fun:

PlayingWithPlays.com

With these notes, I'll see you on the stage, have fun, and break a leg!

SCHOOL, AFTERSCHOOL, and SUMMER classes

I've been teaching these plays as afterschool and summer programs for quite some time. Many people have asked what the program is, therefore, I have put together a basic formula so any teacher or parent can follow and have melodramatic success! As well, many teachers use my books in a variety of ways. You can view the formula and many more resources on my website at: PlayingWithPlays.com

- Brendan

OTHER PLAYS AND FULL LENGTH SCRIPTS

We have over 25 different titles, as well as a full-length play in 4-acts for theatre groups: Shakespeare's Hilarious Tragedies. You can see all of our other titles on our website here: PlayingWithPlays.com/books

As well, you can see a sneak peek at some of those titles at the back of this book.

And, if you ever have any questions, please don't hesitate to ask at: Contact@PlayingWithPlays.com

ROYALTIES

If you have any questions about royalties or performance licenses, here are the basic guidelines:

1) Please contact us! We always LOVE to hear about a school or group performing our books! We would also love to share photos and brag about your program as well! (with your permission, of course)

2) If you are a group and DO NOT charge your kids to be in this production, contact us about discounted copyright fees (one way or another, we will make this work for you!) You are NOT required to buy a book per kid (but, we will still send you some really cool Shakespeare tattoos for your kids!)

3) If you are a group and DO charge your kids to be in the production, (i.e. afterschool program, summer camp) we ask that you purchase a book per kid. Contact us as we will give you a bulk discount (10 books or more) and send some really cool press on Shakespeare tattoos!

4) If you are a group and DO NOT charge the audience to see the plays, please see our website FAQs to see if you are eligible to waive the performance royalties (most performances are eligible).

5) If you are a group and DO charge the audience to see the performance, please see our website FAQs for performance licensing fees (this includes performances for donations and competitions).

Any other questions or comments, please see our website or email us at:

contact@PlayingWithPlays.com

The 15-Minute or so Taming of the Shrew

By William Shakespeare
Creatively modified by
Khara C. Barnhart and Brendan P. Kelso

8-9+ Actors

CAST OF CHARACTERS:

KATHERINA: the SHREW (she's not very nice)

BIANCA: Katherina's younger, super cute sister

BAPTISTA: Katherina and Bianca's father

PETRUCHIO: trying to tame the Shrew (Katherina)

¹GREMIO: old rich dude who wants to marry Bianca

¹GRUMIO: Petruchio's servant (who puts a Gremio AND a Grumio in the same play?!)

LUCENTIO: loves Bianca and pretends to be a teacher named Cambio

HORTENSIO: loves Bianca and pretends to be a musician named Litio

TRANIO: Lucentio's servant who pretends to be Lucentio (confused yet?)

TOWNSFOLK: they live in the town

The same actors can play the following part:
¹GRUMIO and GRUMIO
TOWNSFOLK can be extras as needed

ACT 1 SCENE 1

(enter LUCENTIO and TRANIO)

LUCENTIO: Well, Tranio, my trusty servant, here we are in Padua, Italy! I can't wait to start studying and learn all about philosophy and virtue!

TRANIO: There is such a thing as too much studying, master Lucentio. We need to remember to have fun too! PARTY!

LUCENTIO: Hey look! Here come some of the locals!

(LUCENTIO and TRANIO move to side of stage; Enter BAPTISTA, KATHERINA, BIANCA, HORTENSIO, and GREMIO)

BAPTISTA: Look guys, you know the rules: Bianca can't marry anybody until her older sister, Katherina, is married. That's the plan and I'm sticking to it! If either of you both love Katherina, then please, take her.

KATHERINA: *(Sarcastically)* Wow, thanks, Dad.

HORTENSIO: I wouldn't marry her if she were the last woman on earth.

KATHERINA: And I'd rather scratch your face off than marry you!

TRANIO: *(aside to LUCENTIO)* That wench is stark mad!

BAPTISTA: Enough of this! Bianca, go inside.

BIANCA: Yes, dearest father. My books and instruments shall be my company. *(she exits)*

KATHERINA: *(At BIANCA)* Goody two-shoes.

BAPTISTA: Bianca is so talented in music, instruments, and poetry! I really need to hire some tutors for her. *(KATHERINA rolls her eyes and sighs)* Good-day everyone! *(BAPTISTA exits)*

KATHERINA: *(Very angry)* AGHHHH!!!! I'm outta here

(exits opposite direction from her father)

GREMIO: *(Shudders)* Ugh! How could anyone ever want to marry Katherina?!

HORTENSIO: I don't know, but let's find a husband for her.

GREMIO: A husband? A devil!

HORTENSIO: I say a husband.

GREMIO: I say a devil.

HORTENSIO: Alright, alright! There's got to be a guy out there crazy enough to marry her.

GREMIO: Let's get to it!

(exit GREMIO and HORTENSIO)

LUCENTIO: Oh, Tranio! Sweet Bianca, has stolen my heart! I burn, I pine, I perish! Oh, how I love her!

TRANIO: Whoa, Master! You're getting a little overdramatic, there, Lucentio.

LUCENTIO: Sorry. But my heart is seriously on fire! How am I going to make her fall in love with me if she's not allowed to date anybody? Hmmm...

TRANIO: What if you pretended to be a tutor and went to teach her?

LUCENTIO: YOU ARE BRILLIANT, TRANIO! And because we're new here and no one knows what we look like yet, YOU will pretend to be ME at all the local parties. Quick, let's change clothes.

TRANIO: Here? Now? *(points at audience)* In front of my parents?

LUCENTIO: Yes, Here and now! You can't stop this lovin' feeling! *(Starts singing a love song)*

TRANIO: Please, no singing. I'll do it. *(they exchange hats, socks or jackets)*

LUCENTIO: Perfect! Now while you're pretending to be me, try and get Bianca to marry you. I've got a super confusing plan that I'll tell you about later. Got it?

TRANIO: Huh? I am already confused. But, yeah, got it.

(ALL exit)

ACT 1 SCENE 2

(enter PETRUCHIO and GRUMIO; HORTENSIO enters from opposite side of stage)

HORTENSIO: Petruchio and Grumio! What happy gale blows you to Padua here from old Verona?

PETRUCHIO: Such wind as scatters young men through the world.

GRUMIO: Why don't you tell him why you're REALLY here, Petruchio.

PETRUCHIO: OK, fine. I'm here to find a rich wife. And I mean, RICH!

HORTENSIO: Listen, Petruchio, I know a girl who is very rich, but who is also shrewd and ill-favored. Really, she's just MEAN.

PETRUCHIO: Hortensio, I don't care if she's mean, old, smelly AND ugly. If she's rich, that's all that matters! I come to wive it wealthily in Padua!

GRUMIO: Who is she?

HORTENSIO: Her name is Katherina, renowned in Padua for her scolding tongue.

PETRUCHIO: She sounds awesome! I will not sleep, Hortensio, till I see her. Can we go now? Grumio, go get my stuff! *(GRUMIO exits)*

HORTENSIO: *(to audience)* This is great! I'll take him, but I will disguise myself as a music teacher. That way I can teach Bianca and get her to fall in love with me!

(enter GREMIO and LUCENTIO, disguised as CAMBIO)

HORTENSIO: *(to PETRUCHIO)* Ah, look! That's Gremio. He also wants to marry Bianca, but he doesn't have a chance against me!

(HORTENSIO walks over to GREMIO and LUCENTIO)

HORTENSIO: Hey there, old man! I have some good news! I may have found a husband for Katherina *(points to PETRUCHIO)*...which means Bianca would be fair game.

GREMIO: Have you told him all her faults? *(to PETRUCHIO)* Will you woo this wildcat?

PETRUCHIO: Come on, guys, she can't be that bad. So she has a bad temper. I can deal with it. I am very brave. *(Starts posing like a hero or a bodybuilder; Enter TRANIO pretending to be LUCENTIO)*

TRANIO: Hello gentlemen! Do any of you know the way to Signor Baptista's house? I heard he has a beautiful daughter.

PETRUCHIO: You're not talking about the mean one, right?

TRANIO: Mean? No, no, no... I want the nice one. Bianca.

GREMIO: Sorry, new guy, but Bianca's mine.

HORTENSIO: Not exactly, Gremio, she's actually mine.

TRANIO: Let's just consider her mine, okay?

LUCENTIO: *(to TRANIO, whispering)* You are doing a great job at pretending to be me! Keep it up!

PETRUCHIO: Remember guys, nobody can have Bianca until the elder sister first be wed.

(ALL exit)

ACT 2 SCENE 1

(enter KATHERINA and BIANCA, hands tied)

BIANCA: Katherina, you can't treat me like a slave. Unbind my hands, and I'll give you anything you want!

KATHERINA: I want to know which man you love the most.

BIANCA: I don't like any of them.

KATHERINA: Thou liest. What about Hortensio?

BIANCA: No... if you want him, you shall have him.

KATHERINA: Ew! No thanks. So you like old rich guys like Gremio, then?

BIANCA: You must be joking. Sister Kate, untie my hands.

(KATHERINA sticks out her tongue at BIANCA, who starts crying; Enter BAPTISTA)

BAPTISTA: Girls! Stop this! *(to KATHERINA)* For shame...what the!? What did your sister ever do to you? (BIANCA exits)

KATHERINA: You always take her side! She is your treasure, she must have a husband, I must dance barefoot on her wedding day. Just leave me alone. I will go sit and weep and think of a way to get my revenge! *(KATHERINA exits)*

(enter GREMIO, LUCENTIO disguised as CAMBIO, PETRUCHIO, HORTENSIO disguised as LITIO, and TRANIO disguised as LUCENTIO)

BAPTISTA: Hello gentlemen.

PETRUCHIO: Have you not a daughter called Katherina, fair and virtuous?

BAPTISTA: I have a daughter, sir....called Katherina.

PETRUCHIO: Perfect! I have brought my friend, Litio *(PETRUCHIO pushes HORTENSIO forward towards BAPTISTA)*, who's a totally rockin' musician. I think he'd be an excellent teacher for her.

BAPTISTA: Yeah, sounds great, but Katherina is... well... difficult.

GREMIO: *(to audience)* You can say that again! *(to BAPTISTA)* Baptista, may I present Cambio *(he pushes LUCENTIO towards BAPTISTA)*, a young scholar, who is super duper smart. He'd make a great teacher for Bianca.

BAPTISTA: This is wonderful. Welcome to our household Litio and Cambio. Go on inside! *(HORTENSIO and LUCENTIO exit)*

BAPTISTA: *(to TRANIO)* And who might you be?

TRANIO: I'm Lucentio. I think your daughter Bianca is amazing, and I want to date her!

BAPTISTA: Well, the more, the merrier.

PETRUCHIO: Signor Baptista, I'm in a rush to get married.

BAPTISTA: Okay, if you can get Katherina to love you, you can have her.

PETRUCHIO: I'm a pretty macho guy, Baptista. I'll get her to love me, no problemo.

(enter HORTENSIO disguised as LITIO, stumbling and holding a broken guitar)

BAPTISTA: Why dost thou look so pale? Will my daughter make a good musician?

HORTENSIO: I think she'll sooner prove a soldier! She broke the guitar over my head and called me terrible names!

PETRUCHIO: Sweet! I can't wait to meet this terror of a girl!

BAPTISTA: *(to HORTENSIO)* Go ahead and teach my younger daughter instead. She's much nicer. Petruchio, you stay here and I'll send Katherina out. *(ALL exit except for PETRUCHIO)*

PETRUCHIO: *(to Audience)* This ought to be good!!

(enter KATHERINA)

PETRUCHIO: Good morrow Kate; for that's your name, I hear. Kate... Kate... Kate!

KATHERINA: It's Katherina.

PETRUCHIO: You lie, in faith, for you are called plain Kate, and bonny Kate, and sometimes Kate the curst... but you are my super-dainty Kate, and I am going to marry you.

KATHERINA: *(Starts laughing hysterically)* Riiiiiiiiiiiiiiiiiight. And I'm the queen of England.

PETRUCHIO: Oh, come on, sweet Kitty "Kat." Here.... kitty, kitty, kitty...

KATHERINA: Hiss!!

PETRUCHIO: Come, come, you wasp. I'faith, you are too angry.

KATHERINA: If I be waspish, best beware my sting! *(she swings at PETRUCHIO)*

PETRUCHIO: Okay, I get it. No more animal references. But you will be my wife; I am born to tame you, Kate!

(enter BAPTISTA, GREMIO and TRANIO disguised as LUCENTIO)

BAPTISTA: So, how'd it go?

PETRUCHIO: Great!

KATHERINA: Terrible!

PETRUCHIO: *(Holds hand over KATHERINA'S mouth so she can't talk)* We've decided that Sunday is the wedding day.

BAPTISTA: Wonderful! I'll start the preparations.

PETRUCHIO: And I'll go buy fancy clothes and rings. *(KATHERINA elbows PETRUCHIO in the side)* Woo-hoo! *(PETRUCHIO exits one direction, while KATHERINA storms off stage in the opposite direction)*

TRANIO: Alright! Now we can finally talk about Bianca! I love her so!

GREMIO: I saw her first!! Thou canst not love so dear as I.

TRANIO: Yes I CANST!

BAPTISTA: Look, it's simple: whoever has the most money gets Bianca.

GREMIO: I have tons of cash! *(Starts throwing dollars all over the stage and in the audience)*

TRANIO: I have more! *(Pulls out his credit card)*

BAPTISTA: *(Grabs credit card)* Okay then, Lucentio, you get Bianca! You can marry her after Katherina's wedding, IF you can get your father to pay the dowry. If not, then Gremio can have her. *(BAPTISTA exits)*

GREMIO: Good luck, daddy's boy!

(ALL exit)

ACT 3 SCENE 1

(enter HORTENSIO disguised as LITIO, LUCENTIO disguised as CAMBIO and BIANCA)

LUCENTIO: Ok, Bianca, let's hit the books! I have so much to teach you today.

HORTENSIO: I don't think so, Cambio. Music first, then you can get to your boring books...SNORE!

BIANCA: Let me choose; I'll learn my lessons as I please myself. Books first.

(LUCENTIO pumps his fist in the air as a "winner," while HORTENSIO walks to the side of the stage and pouts)

LUCENTIO: *(Opens a large book)* THIS, sweet Bianca, is Latin.

BIANCA: Got it. Next? *(she turns to HORTENSIO)* What'cha got, Litio?

HORTENSIO: THIS, dear Bianca, is Rock and Roll. *(begins playing on his guitar like a rock musician and gets carried away)*

BIANCA: Got it. Farewell, sweet masters both. I must be gone. *(BIANCA exits)*

HORTENSIO and LUCENTIO: Bye Bianca!

(they give each other dirty looks and exit opposite sides of the stage)

ACT 3 SCENE 2

(enter BAPTISTA, GREMIO, TRANIO disguised as LUCENTIO, KATHERINA, BIANCA, and LUCENTIO disguised as CAMBIO)

BAPTISTA: *(to TRANIO)* Oh, Lucentio, today's the day that Katherine and Petruchio should be married, but Petruchio is nowhere to be found!

KATHERINA: I told you, he was a frantic fool!

TRANIO: Patience, good Katherine, and Baptista too. He'll be here, don't worry!

KATHERINA: What-EVER! *(she exits)*

BIANCA: *(looks offstage)* You guys will never believe this! Petruchio is coming but his pants are inside out, his boots are mismatched and falling apart, and he's got an old rusty sword! Oh, but he's got a new hat! Look! *(PETRUCHIO enters looking like a clown).*

PETRUCHIO: Who's ready for a wedding?! *(looks around)* But where is Kate? Where is my love?

BAPTISTA: You know this is your wedding day...right? You will not marry her looking like that!

PETRUCHIO: Oh yes I will! Better get to the church! *(PETRUCHIO exits)*

BAPTISTA: I better go too. Come on, Gremio! *(BAPTISTA, BIANCA, and GREMIO exit)*

TRANIO: *(to LUCENTIO)* Good news, Lucentio! Baptista said I –er... YOU could marry Bianca, as long as your father can provide the money. I will write a pretend letter from your dad so you can marry sweet Bianca right away!

LUCENTIO: Awesome!

(enter GREMIO)

GREMIO: That was the weirdest wedding I've ever been to! Petruchio yelled like a crazy man, knocked down the priest, and scared everyone half to death! I've never seen anything like it!

LUCENTIO: Here they come!

(enter PETRUCHIO, KATHERINA, BIANCA, BAPTISTA, and HORTENSIO)

PETRUCHIO: Friends, I thank you for showing up, but now we must go. Come on, Kate!

KATHERINA: But I'm hungry and there's this huge feast waiting! Now, if you love me, stay.

PETRUCHIO: Ahhhh... NO! We're leaving!

KATHERINA: Oh, you mean...terrible...rotten worm!

PETRUCHIO: *(mocking her)* I know you are but what am I?

KATHERINA: Stop it!

PETRUCHIO: Fine! *(to everyone else onstage)* You all go party, be mad and merry. Kate belongs to me now, and I'm taking her home. *(PETRUCHIO grabs KATHERINA and exits; KATHERINA screams until they are offstage; Everyone onstage is shocked and silent)*

LUCENTIO: *(to BIANCA)* Mistress, what's your opinion of your sister?

BIANCA: That being mad herself, she's madly mated.

BAPTISTA: Well, let's not waste the wedding food! Come, gentlemen, let's go eat!

(ALL exit)

ACT 4 SCENE 1

(enter GRUMIO)

GRUMIO: *(to the audience)* Katherina and Petruchio will be here any second.

(enter PETRUCHIO and KATHERINA)

PETRUCHIO: Where be these knaves? Where are my servants?

GRUMIO: I think they're in the kitchen cooking your welcome home meal.

PETRUCHIO: Go and fetch my supper. NOW!

(GRUMIO exits)

PETRUCHIO: Sit down, Kate, and welcome. *(Starts sniffing the air and then yells off stage)* You villains burned the meat! I can smell it from here! Yuck! Throw it away! You heedless joltheads and unmannered slaves!

KATHERINA: It smells fine to me...and I'm so hungry!

PETRUCHIO: I tell thee, Kate, 'twas burnt and dried away. No dinner for us tonight. Come on, let's go to bed. *(they exit together then PETRUCHIO reenters alone)*

PETRUCHIO: *(to audience)* This is the "taming" part of the "Taming of the Shrew." Get it? She ate no meat today, nor none will eat. Last night she slept not, nor to-night she shall not. I'm going to make her miserable until she becomes a better person. This will be so fun!

(PETRUCHIO exits)

ACT 4 SCENE 2

(enter TRANIO disguised as LUCENTIO and HORTENSIO disguised as LITIO)

TRANIO: I think that Bianca is totally in love with me, don't you?

HORTENSIO: Ha! You think so, Lucentio? Just watch this...

(enter BIANCA and LUCENTIO disguised as CAMBIO)

BIANCA: *(to LUCENTIO)* What are we going to study today?

LUCENTIO: My favorite book: The Art to Love!

BIANCA: Sweet! I love love!

LUCENTIO: And I love you! *(big hug)*

HORTENSIO: *(to TRANIO)* Now, tell me, I pray, what were you saying about Bianca being in love with you?

TRANIO: Aghhh...O despiteful love! Guess I was wrong.

HORTENSIO: Okay, listen. I am not Litio, nor a musician. My real name is Hortensio.

TRANIO: Well, Hortensio, it looks like Bianca loves that Cambio guy. Should we give up?

HORTENSIO: Yep! I'm going to marry a wealthy widow in town. And so farewell. *(HORTENSIO exits)*

TRANIO: Hey lovebirds! Hortensio's off to go to marry some rich widow.

BIANCA: God give him joy!

LUCENTIO: *(to BIANCA)* Now you're all mine!

BIANCA: Oh, Cambio! I mean...Lucentio. *(giggles)* I'm still getting used to all this "disguise" stuff.

TRANIO: Lucentio, look at this. *(Pulls a letter out of his pocket)* I think I've got your dad's handwriting down. This letter should convince Baptista that your dad will pay for everything so you can marry Bianca.

LUCENTIO: Thanks, man...you're the best!

TRANIO: Oh, don't I know it. Come on!

(LUCENTIO, TRANIO, and BIANCA exit)

ACT 4 SCENE 3

(enter KATHERINA and GRUMIO)

KATHERINA: Please, please, please? Won't you give me any food? I am SOOOOO hungry!

GRUMIO: I dare not for my life.

(enter PETRUCHIO and HORTENSIO)

KATHERINA: But I'm starving!! If you don't feed me, I'll die!

PETRUCHIO: Oh, don't be so dramatic! This isn't Romeo and Juliet – no one's dying in this play.

HORTENSIO: *(to PETRUCHIO)* Shouldn't you feed her? Aren't you going too far in this "taming" business?

PETRUCHIO: Don't you worry about it! O Grumio, Grumio! Wherefore art thou, Grumio?

GRUMIO: Uh, I'm right here, Petruchio.

PETRUCHIO: Did the new cap and gown I ordered for sweet Kate arrive? *(Gives an evil grin to the audience)*

GRUMIO: Yes, come with me, and I'll show you.

(exit PETRUCHIO, KATHERINA, and GRUMIO)

HORTENSIO: *(to Audience)* I've got a bad feeling about this.

(enter PETRUCHIO, KATHERINA, and GRUMIO)

PETRUCHIO: That hat was way too small for your big head. It's like a toy or a baby's cap. Throw it out!

KATHERINA: I like the cap, and I will have it.

PETRUCHIO: When you are gentle, you shall have one.

KATHERINA: I am no child. Quit treating me like a baby!!

PETRUCHIO: Then quit whining like a baby! You know what? That dress was really ugly. *(to GRUMIO)* Throw that out too!

KATHERINA: Are you nuts! I never saw a better-fashioned gown.

PETRUCHIO: Sorry, Kate. We'll head back to your father's house in our plain old, dirty clothes. In fact, we'll not go today. We'll go see your dad tomorrow.

KATHERINA: Aghhhhhhhhhhhhhhhh! I am sooooo mad!!!!!!!! *(Starts stomping her feet; PETRUCHIO, KATHERINA, and GRUMIO exit)*

HORTENSIO: *(to Audience)* Who does he think he is, the king? I'm glad I don't live here!

(HORTENSIO exits)

ACT 4 SCENE 4

(enter BAPTISTA, TRANIO disguised as LUCENTIO, and LUCENTIO disguised as CAMBIO)

TRANIO: *(Hands the letter to BAPTISTA)* Here's the letter from my dad.

BAPTISTA: Thanks! Yes, he does say that money is no object. Well then, the match is made and all is done. You may marry my daughter, Lucentio.

TRANIO: Let's go back to my house and sign the contract! *(TRANIO gives LUCENTIO a "thumbs up")*

(BAPTISTA and TRANIO exit)

LUCENTIO: *(to the audience)* There is an old priest waiting at the church to marry us right now. Bianca will be pleased. We're going to be together forever! Yippee!

(LUCENTIO exits)

ACT 4 SCENE 5

(enter PETRUCHIO, KATHERINA, HORTENSIO, and GRUMIO)

PETRUCHIO: What a great night for traveling to your dad's! How bright and goodly shines the moon!

KATHERINA: The moon? The sun! It's DAYTIME!

PETRUCHIO: I say it is the moon that shines so bright.

KATHERINA: I know it is the sun that shines so bright.

HORTENSIO: *(to KATHERINA)* Just say what he wants you to say, or we'll never get out of here!

PETRUCHIO: I say it is the moon.

KATHERINA: *(looks at HORTENSIO and sighs loudly)* Fine. I know it is the moon.

PETRUCHIO: Then you lie. It is the blessed sun.

KATHERINA: Are you kidding me?! This is ridiculous! Okay, you win, it's the sun!

PETRUCHIO: That's what I like to hear! Come on, we better get going!

(shoots a big happy grin to the audience; ALL exit)

ACT 5 SCENE 1

(enter PETRUCHIO, KATHERINA, and GRUMIO)

PETRUCHIO: Not too much farther to your dad's place.

(enter BAPTISTA)

BAPTISTA: Welcome back, newlyweds! Have you seen Bianca? I can't find her anywhere!

(enter LUCENTIO and BIANCA)

BIANCA: Hi Dad!

LUCENTIO: Yeah, hi Dad!

BAPTISTA: What?!

BIANCA: We got married. *(giggles)*

BAPTISTA: *(to LUCENTIO)* But you're Cambio, the poor teacher.

BIANCA: Cambio is changed into Lucentio! SO cool. I love him!

BAPTISTA: I need to sit down. Let's go inside and you can explain this all to me.

(everyone exits except KATHERINA and PETRUCHIO)

KATHERINA: Husband, let's follow to see what happens!

PETRUCHIO: First kiss me, Kate, and we will.

KATHERINA: Ew. Gross. No way.

PETRUCHIO: Well, I tried. Come on!

(ALL exit)

ACT 5 SCENE 2

(enter LUCENTIO, PETRUCHIO, BAPTISTA, HORTENSIO, TRANIO, and GRUMIO)

LUCENTIO: What a great feast!

BAPTISTA: Both my lovely daughters are married! Although Petruchio, you did get stuck with the shrew!

PETRUCHIO: Well, I say no. She's really quite charming and agreeable.

HORTENSIO: Yeah, right. *(the men laugh)*

PETRUCHIO: Well, how about a challenge, then? Let's each one send unto his wife; and he whose wife comes right away, wins!

LUCENTIO: You're on! I bet a hundred crowns.

HORTENSIO: Me too!

PETRUCHIO: Fantastic. Who shall begin?

LUCENTIO: I will. Grumio – go and get Bianca.

(GRUMIO exits)

BAPTISTA: I'm sure Bianca will come right away!

(GRUMIO enters)

GRUMIO: Sorry, Lucentio, Bianca says that she is busy, and she cannot come.

(the men all groan and pat LUCENTIO on the back)

HORTENSIO: My turn! Grumio – go and get my wife.

(GRUMIO exits)

PETRUCHIO: Let's see how fast she'll come...

(GRUMIO enters)

GRUMIO: *(to HORTENSIO)* Your wife thinks this is a joke. She will not come. Actually, she said she's going home and will see you later.

(the men all groan and laugh and pat HORTENSIO on the back)

PETRUCHIO: My turn. Grumio – go and get my Kate!

(Grumio exits)

HORTENSIO: This will never happen.

(enter KATHERINA)

KATHERINA: Yes, dear?

(all the men have shocked looks on their faces)

PETRUCHIO: Where is your sister?

KATHERINA: Sitting by the parlor fire.

PETRUCHIO: Go and get her, please.

(KATHERINA exits)

LUCENTIO and HORTENSIO: Whoooooooa.

BAPTISTA: Petruchio wins the bet! Now, what have you done with my daughter? That couldn't be my Katherina!

(enter KATHERINA and BIANCA)

PETRUCHIO: Kate, please explain to Bianca how to be a good wife.

BIANCA: Seriously? *(she starts laughing)*

KATHERINA: *(to BIANCA, with a wink and a smile)* No, I've got this. *(to everyone)* Ahem! Thy husband is thy lord, thy life, thy keeper, and we ladies should be nice and LOVE him. *(to PETRUCHIO)* How'd I do?

PETRUCHIO: Couldn't have said it better myself. Come on, wonderful wife, let's go to sleep. Good-night everybody!

(PETRUCHIO and KATHERINA exit)

HORTENSIO: I can't believe he tamed a curst shrew!

LUCENTIO: Totally unbelievable, but true!

(ALL exit)

THE END

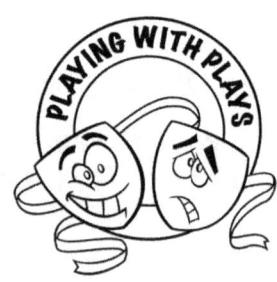

NOTES

The 20-Minute or so Taming of the Shrew

By William Shakespeare
Creatively modified by
Khara C. Barnhart and Brendan P. Kelso

10-13 Actors

CAST OF CHARACTERS:

KATHERINA: the SHREW (she's not very nice)

BIANCA: Katherina's younger, super cute sister

[1]BAPTISTA: Katherina and Bianca's father

PETRUCHIO: trying to tame the Shrew (Katherina)

[2]GREMIO: old rich dude who wants to marry Bianca

[3]GRUMIO: Petruchio's servant (who puts a Gremio AND a Grumio in the same play?!)

LUCENTIO: loves Bianca and pretends to be a teacher named Cambio

HORTENSIO: loves Bianca and pretends to be a musician named Litio

TRANIO: Lucentio's servant who pretends to be Lucentio (confused yet?)

[2]VINCENTIO: Lucentio's dad

[3]MERCHANT: pretends to be Lucentio's dad

WIDOW: a rich widow

[1]CURTIS: one of Petruchio's servants

TOWNSFOLK: they live in the town

The same actors can play the following parts:
[1]BAPTISTA and CURTIS
[2]VINCENTIO and GREMIO
[3]GRUMIO and the MERCHANT
TOWNSFOLK can be extras as needed

ACT 1 SCENE 1

(enter LUCENTIO and TRANIO)

LUCENTIO: Well, Tranio, my trusty servant, here we are in Padua, Italy! I can't wait to start studying and learn all about philosophy and virtue!

TRANIO: There is such a thing as too much studying, master Lucentio. We need to remember to have fun too! PARTY!

LUCENTIO: Hey look! Here come some of the locals!

(LUCENTIO and TRANIO move to side of stage; Enter BAPTISTA, KATHERINA, BIANCA, HORTENSIO, and GREMIO)

BAPTISTA: Look guys, you know the rules: Bianca can't marry anybody until her older sister, Katherina, is married. That's the plan and I'm sticking to it! If either of you both love Katherina, then please, take her.

KATHERINA: *(Sarcastically)* Wow, thanks, Dad.

HORTENSIO: I wouldn't marry her if she were the last woman on earth.

KATHERINA: And I'd rather scratch your face off than marry you!

TRANIO: *(aside to LUCENTIO)* That wench is stark mad!

BAPTISTA: Enough of this! Bianca, go inside.

BIANCA: Yes, dearest father. My books and instruments shall be my company. *(she exits)*

KATHERINA: *(At BIANCA)* Goody two-shoes.

BAPTISTA: Bianca is so talented in music, instruments, and poetry! I really need to hire some tutors for her. *(KATHERINA rolls her eyes and sighs)* Good-day everyone! *(BAPTISTA exits)*

KATHERINA: *(very angry)* AGHHHH!!!! I'm outta here *(exits opposite direction from her father)*

GREMIO: *(Shudders)* Ugh! How could anyone ever want to marry Katherina?!

HORTENSIO: I don't know, but let's find a husband for her.

GREMIO: A husband? A devil!

HORTENSIO: I say a husband.

GREMIO: I say a devil.

HORTENSIO: Alright, alright! There's got to be a guy out there crazy enough to marry her.

GREMIO: Let's get to it!

(exit GREMIO and HORTENSIO)

LUCENTIO: Oh, Tranio! Sweet Bianca, has stolen my heart! I burn, I pine, I perish! Oh, how I love her!

TRANIO: Whoa, Master! You're getting a little overdramatic, there, Lucentio.

LUCENTIO: Sorry. But my heart is seriously on fire! How am I going to make her fall in love with me if she's not allowed to date anybody? Hmmm...

TRANIO: What if you pretended to be a tutor and went to teach her?

LUCENTIO: YOU ARE BRILLIANT, TRANIO! And because we're new here and no one knows what we look like yet, YOU will pretend to be ME at all the local parties. Quick, let's change clothes.

TRANIO: Here? Now? *(points at audience)* In front of my parents?

LUCENTIO: Yes, Here and now! You can't stop this lovin' feeling! *(Starts singing a love song)*

TRANIO: Please, no singing. I'll do it. *(they exchange hats, socks or jackets)*

LUCENTIO: Perfect! Now while you're pretending to be me, try and get Bianca to marry you. I've got a super confusing plan that I'll tell you about later. Got it?

TRANIO: Huh? I am already confused. But, yeah, got it.

(ALL exit)

ACT 1 SCENE 2

(enter PETRUCHIO and GRUMIO; HORTENSIO enters from opposite side of stage)

HORTENSIO: Petruchio and Grumio! What happy gale blows you to Padua here from old Verona?

PETRUCHIO: Such wind as scatters young men through the world.

GRUMIO: Why don't you tell him why you're REALLY here, Petruchio.

PETRUCHIO: OK, fine. I'm here to find a rich wife. And I mean, RICH!

HORTENSIO: Listen, Petruchio, I know a girl who is very rich, but who is also shrewd and ill-favored. Really, she's just MEAN.

PETRUCHIO: Hortensio, I don't care if she's mean, old, smelly AND ugly. If she's rich, that's all that matters! I come to wive it wealthily in Padua!

GRUMIO: Who is she?

HORTENSIO: Her name is Katherina, renowned in Padua for her scolding tongue.

PETRUCHIO: She sounds awesome! I will not sleep, Hortensio, till I see her. Can we go now?

HORTENSIO: *(to audience)* This is great! I'll take him, but I will disguise myself as a music teacher. That way I can teach Bianca and get her to fall in love with me!

(enter GREMIO and LUCENTIO, disguised as a teacher, CAMBIO)

HORTENSIO: *(to PETRUCHIO and GRUMIO)* Ah, look! That's Gremio. He also wants to marry Bianca, but he doesn't have a chance against me!

(HORTENSIO walks over to GREMIO and LUCENTIO)

HORTENSIO: Hey there, old man! I have some good news! I may have found a husband for Katherina *(points to PETRUCHIO)*...which means Bianca would be fair game.

GREMIO: Have you told him all her faults? *(to PETRUCHIO)* Will you woo this wildcat?

PETRUCHIO: Come on, guys, she can't be that bad. So she has a bad temper. I can deal with it. I am very brave. *(Starts posing like a hero or a bodybuilder; Enter TRANIO pretending to be LUCENTIO)*

TRANIO: Hello gentlemen! Do any of you know the way to Signor Baptista's house? I heard he has a beautiful daughter.

PETRUCHIO: You're not talking about the mean one, right?

TRANIO: Mean? No, no, no... I want the nice one. Bianca.

GREMIO: Sorry, new guy, but Bianca's mine.

HORTENSIO: Not exactly, Gremio, she's actually mine.

TRANIO: Let's just consider her mine, okay?

LUCENTIO: *(to TRANIO, whispering)* You are doing a great job at pretending to be me! Keep it up!

PETRUCHIO: Remember guys, nobody can have Bianca until the elder sister first be wed.

(ALL exit)

ACT 2 SCENE 1

(enter KATHERINA and BIANCA, hands tied)

BIANCA: Katherina, you can't treat me like a slave. Unbind my hands, and I'll give you anything you want!

KATHERINA: I want to know which man you love the most.

BIANCA: I don't like any of them.

KATHERINA: Thou liest. What about Hortensio?

BIANCA: No... if you want him, you shall have him.

KATHERINA: Ew! No thanks. So you like old rich guys like Gremio, then?

BIANCA: You must be joking. Sister Kate, untie my hands.

(KATHERINA sticks out her tongue at BIANCA, who starts crying; Enter BAPTISTA)

BAPTISTA: Girls! Stop this! *(to KATHERINA)* For shame...what the!? ...What did your sister ever do to you? *(BIANCA exits)*

KATHERINA: You always take her side! She is your treasure, she must have a husband, I must dance barefoot on her wedding day. Just leave me alone. I will go sit and weep and think of a way to get my revenge!

(KATHERINA exits)

(enter GREMIO, LUCENTIO disguised as CAMBIO, PETRUCHIO, HORTENSIO disguised as LITIO, and TRANIO disguised as LUCENTIO)

BAPTISTA: Hello gentlemen.

PETRUCHIO: Have you not a daughter called Katherina, fair and virtuous?

BAPTISTA: I have a daughter, sir....called Katherina.

PETRUCHIO: Perfect! I have brought my friend, Litio *(PETRUCHIO pushes HORTENSIO forward towards BAPTISTA)*, who's a totally rockin' musician. I think he'd be an excellent teacher for her.

BAPTISTA: Yeah, sounds great, but Katherina is... well... difficult.

GREMIO: *(to audience)* You can say that again! *(to BAPTISTA)* Baptista, may I present Cambio *(he pushes LUCENTIO towards BAPTISTA)*, a young scholar, who is super duper smart. He'd make a great teacher for Bianca.

BAPTISTA: This is wonderful. Welcome to our household Litio and Cambio. Go on inside! *(HORTENSIO and LUCENTIO exit)*

BAPTISTA: *(to TRANIO)* And who might you be?

TRANIO: I'm Lucentio. I think your daughter Bianca is amazing, and I want to date her!

BAPTISTA: Well, the more, the merrier.

PETRUCHIO: Signor Baptista, I'm in a rush to get married.

BAPTISTA: Okay, if you can get Katherina to love you, you can have her.

PETRUCHIO: I'm a pretty macho guy, Baptista. I'll get her to love me, no problemo.

(enter HORTENSIO disguised as LITIO, stumbling and holding a broken guitar)

BAPTISTA: Why dost thou look so pale? Will my daughter make a good musician?

HORTENSIO: I think she'll sooner prove a soldier! She broke the guitar over my head and called me terrible names!

PETRUCHIO: Sweet! I can't wait to meet this terror of a girl!

BAPTISTA: *(to HORTENSIO)* Go ahead and teach my younger daughter instead. She's much nicer. Petruchio, you stay here and I'll send Katherina out. *(ALL exit except for PETRUCHIO)*

PETRUCHIO: *(to Audience)* This ought to be good!!

(enter KATHERINA)

PETRUCHIO: Good morrow Kate; for that's your name, I hear. Kate...Kate...Kate!

KATHERINA: It's Katherina.

PETRUCHIO: You lie, in faith, for you are called plain Kate, and bonny Kate, and sometimes Kate the curst... but you are my super-dainty Kate, and I am going to marry you.

KATHERINA: *(Starts laughing hysterically)* Riiiiiiiiiiiiiiiiiight. And I'm the queen of England.

PETRUCHIO: Oh, come on, sweet Kitty "Kat." Here.... kitty, kitty, kitty...

KATHERINA: Hiss!!

PETRUCHIO: Come, come, you wasp. I'faith, you are too angry.

KATHERINA: If I be waspish, best beware my sting! *(she swings at PETRUCHIO)*

PETRUCHIO: Okay, I get it. No more animal references. But you will be my wife; I am born to tame you, Kate!

(enter BAPTISTA, GREMIO and TRANIO disguised as LUCENTIO)

BAPTISTA: So, how'd it go?

PETRUCHIO: Great!

KATHERINA: Terrible!

PETRUCHIO: *(Holds hand over KATHERINA'S mouth so she can't talk)* We've decided that Sunday is the wedding day.

BAPTISTA: Wonderful! I'll start the preparations.

PETRUCHIO: And I'll go buy fancy clothes and rings. *(KATHERINA elbows PETRUCHIO in the side)* Woo-hoo! *(PETRUCHIO exits one direction, while KATHERINA storms off stage in the opposite direction)*

TRANIO: Alright! Now we can finally talk about Bianca! I love her so!

GREMIO: I saw her first!! Thou canst not love so dear as I.

TRANIO: Yes I CANST!

BAPTISTA: Look, it's simple: whoever has the most money gets Bianca.

GREMIO: I have tons of cash! *(Starts throwing dollars all over the stage and in the audience)*

TRANIO: I have more! *(Pulls out his credit card)*

BAPTISTA: *(Grabs credit card)* Okay then, Lucentio, you get Bianca! You can marry her after Katherina's wedding, IF you can get your father to pay the dowry. If not, then Gremio can have her. *(BAPTISTA exits)*

GREMIO: Good luck, daddy's boy! *(exits)*

TRANIO: *(to audience)* I'd say I've been doing a pretty good job pretending to be Lucentio. But now I have to find someone to pretend to be my dad... I mean Lucentio's dad!

(TRANIO exits)

ACT 3 SCENE 1

(enter HORTENSIO disguised as LITIO, LUCENTIO disguised as CAMBIO and BIANCA)

LUCENTIO: Ok, Bianca, let's hit the books! I have so much to teach you today!

HORTENSIO: I don't think so, Cambio. Music first, then you can get to your boring books...SNORE!

BIANCA: Let me choose; I'll learn my lessons as I please myself. Books first.

(LUCENTIO pumps his fist in the air as a "winner," while HORTENSIO walks to the side of the stage and pouts)

LUCENTIO: *(Opens a large book)* THIS, sweet Bianca, is Latin.

BIANCA: Got it. Next? *(she turns to HORTENSIO)* What'cha got, Litio?

HORTENSIO: THIS, dear Bianca, is Rock and Roll. *(begins playing on his guitar like a rock musician and gets carried away)*

BIANCA: Got it. Farewell, sweet masters both. I must be gone. *(BIANCA exits)*

HORTENSIO and LUCENTIO: Bye Bianca!

(they give each other dirty looks and exit opposite sides of the stage)

ACT 3 SCENE 2

(enter BAPTISTA, GREMIO, TRANIO disguised as LUCENTIO, KATHERINA, BIANCA, and LUCENTIO disguised as CAMBIO)

BAPTISTA: *(to TRANIO)* Oh, Lucentio, today's the day that Katherine and Petruchio should be married, but Petruchio is nowhere to be found!

KATHERINA: I told you, he was a frantic fool!

TRANIO: Patience, good Katherine, and Baptista too. He'll be here, don't worry!

KATHERINA: What-EVER! *(she exits)*

BIANCA: *(looks offstage)* Petruchio is coming but his pants are inside out, his boots are mismatched and falling apart, and he's got an old rusty sword! Oh, but he's got a new hat! Look! *(PETRUCHIO enters looking like a clown, with GRUMIO)*.

PETRUCHIO: Who's ready for a wedding?! *(looks around)* But where is Kate? Where is my love?

BAPTISTA: You know this is your wedding day...right? You will not marry her looking like that!

PETRUCHIO: Oh yes I will! Better get to the church! *(PETRUCHIO and GRUMIO exit)*

BAPTISTA: I better go too. Come on, Gremio! *(BAPTISTA, BIANCA, and GREMIO exit)*

TRANIO: *(to LUCENTIO)* Good news, Lucentio! Baptista said I –er... YOU could marry Bianca, as long as your father can provide the money. I will get a man to pretend to be your dad, Vincentio, so you can marry sweet Bianca right away!

LUCENTIO: Awesome plan!

(enter GREMIO)

GREMIO: That was the weirdest wedding I've ever been to! Petruchio yelled like a crazy man, knocked down the priest, and scared everyone half to death! I've never seen anything like it!

LUCENTIO: Here they come!

(enter PETRUCHIO, KATHERINA, BIANCA, BAPTISTA, HORTENSIO, and GRUMIO)

PETRUCHIO: Friends, I thank you for showing up, but now we must go. Come on, Kate!

KATHERINA: But I'm hungry and there's this huge feast waiting! Now, if you love me, stay.

PETRUCHIO: Ahhhh... NO! We're leaving!

KATHERINA: Oh, you mean...terrible...rotten worm!

PETRUCHIO: *(mocking her)* I know you are but what am I?

KATHERINA: Stop it!

PETRUCHIO: Fine! *(to everyone else onstage)* You all go party, be mad and merry. Kate belongs to me now, and I'm taking her home. *(PETRUCHIO grabs KATHERINA and exits, followed by GRUMIO; KATHERINA screams until they are offstage; everyone onstage is shocked and silent)*

LUCENTIO: *(to BIANCA)* Mistress, what's your opinion of your sister?

BIANCA: That being mad herself, she's madly mated.

BAPTISTA: Well, let's not waste the wedding food! Come, gentlemen, let's go eat!

(ALL exit)

ACT 4 SCENE 1

(enter GRUMIO and CURTIS)

CURTIS: Is my master Petruchio and his wife coming, Grumio?

GRUMIO: They'll be here any second. We're all tired and hungry.

(enter PETRUCHIO and KATHERINA)

PETRUCHIO: Where is my servant, Curtis?

CURTIS: Here, here, sir!

PETRUCHIO: *(mockingly)* "Here, sir. Here sir!" You loggerheaded and unpolished fool! Go and fetch my supper. NOW!

(CURTIS and GRUMIO exit)

PETRUCHIO: Sit down, Kate, and welcome. *(Starts sniffing the air and then yells off stage)* You villains burned the meat! I can smell it from here! Yuck! Throw it away! You heedless joltheads and unmannered slaves!

KATHERINA: It smells fine to me...and I'm so hungry!

PETRUCHIO: I tell thee, Kate, 'twas burnt and dried away. No dinner for us tonight. Come on, let's go to bed. *(they exit together then PETRUCHIO reenters alone)*

PETRUCHIO: *(to audience)* This is the "taming" part of the "Taming of the Shrew." Get it? She ate no meat today, nor none will eat. Last night she slept not, nor to-night she shall not. I'm going to make her miserable until she becomes a better person. This will be so fun!

(PETRUCHIO exits)

ACT 4 SCENE 2

(enter TRANIO disguised as LUCENTIO and HORTENSIO disguised as LITIO)

TRANIO: I think that Bianca is totally in love with me, don't you?

HORTENSIO: Ha! You think so, Lucentio? Just watch....

(enter BIANCA and LUCENTIO disguised as CAMBIO)

BIANCA: *(to LUCENTIO)* What are we going to study today?

LUCENTIO: My favorite book: The Art to Love!

BIANCA: Sweet! I love love!

LUCENTIO: And I love you!

HORTENSIO: *(to TRANIO)* Now, tell me, I pray, what were you saying about Bianca being in love with you?

TRANIO: Aghhh...O despiteful love! Guess I was wrong.

HORTENSIO: Okay, listen. I am not Litio, nor a musician. My real name is Hortensio.

TRANIO: Well, Hortensio, it looks like Bianca loves that Cambio guy. Should we give up?

HORTENSIO: Yep! I'm going to marry a wealthy widow in town. And so farewell. *(HORTENSIO exits)*

TRANIO: Hey lovebirds! Hortensio's off to go to marry some rich widow.

BIANCA: God give him joy!

LUCENTIO: *(to BIANCA)* Now you're all mine!

BIANCA: Oh, Cambio! I mean...Lucentio. *(giggles)* I'm still getting used to all this "disguise" stuff.

TRANIO: Hey look! *(points offstage)* An old merchant is coming this way. He looks like the perfect guy to pretend to be your dad! You guys get out of here and leave this to me!

(LUCENTIO and BIANCA exit; Enter the MERCHANT)

TRANIO: Hello there! What brings you to Padua?

MERCHANT: Just passing through on business.

TRANIO: *(overly dramatic)* You know, it can be dangerous in this part of the world. If you pretend to be my father, Vincentio, you can stay at my house while you're here and I'll keep you safe. How does that sound?

MERCHANT: Sounds like a plan!

TRANIO: Perfect.

(ALL exit)

ACT 4 SCENE 3

(enter KATHERINA and GRUMIO)

KATHERINA: Please, please, please? Won't you give me any food? I am SOOOOO hungry!

GRUMIO: I dare not for my life.

(enter PETRUCHIO and HORTENSIO)

KATHERINA: But I'm starving!! If you don't feed me, I'll die!

PETRUCHIO: Oh, don't be so dramatic! This isn't Romeo and Juliet – no one's dying in this play.

HORTENSIO: *(to PETRUCHIO)* Shouldn't you feed her? Aren't you going too far in this "taming" business?

PETRUCHIO: Don't you worry about it! O Grumio, Grumio! Wherefore art thou, Grumio?

GRUMIO: Uh, I'm right here, Petruchio.

PETRUCHIO: Did the new cap and gown I ordered for sweet Kate arrive? *(Gives an evil grin to the audience)*

GRUMIO: Yes, come with me, and I'll show you.

(exit PETRUCHIO, KATHERINA, and GRUMIO)

HORTENSIO: *(to Audience)* I've got a bad feeling about this.

(enter PETRUCHIO, KATHERINA, and GRUMIO)

PETRUCHIO: That hat was way too small for your big head. It's like a toy or a baby's cap. Throw it out!

KATHERINA: I like the cap, and I will have it.

PETRUCHIO: When you are gentle, you shall have one.

KATHERINA: I am no child. Quit treating me like a baby!!

PETRUCHIO: Then quit whining like a baby! You know what? That dress was really ugly. *(to GRUMIO)* Throw that out too!

KATHERINA: Are you nuts! I never saw a better-fashioned gown.

PETRUCHIO: Sorry, Kate. We'll head back to your father's house in our plain old, dirty clothes. In fact, we'll not go today. We'll go see your dad tomorrow.

KATHERINA: Aghhhhhhhhhhhhhhhhh! I am sooooo mad!!!!!!!! *(Starts stomping her feet; PETRUCHIO, KATHERINA, and GRUMIO exit)*

HORTENSIO: *(to Audience)* Who does he think he is, the king? I'm glad I don't live here!

(HORTENSIO exits)

(enter TRANIO disguised as LUCENTIO and the MERCHANT disguised as VINCENTIO)

TRANIO: Ready?

MERCHANT: Yes I am...son! From now on, I am your father whose name is Vincentio.

(enter BAPTISTA and LUCENTIO disguised as CAMBIO)

MERCHANT: Good day, Baptista! My son tells me he's in love with your daughter, Bianca, and wants to marry her. I am content to let the wedding happen.

BAPTISTA: Thanks! If you can show me the money, then the match is made and all is done. Your son shall have my daughter with consent.

TRANIO: Let's go back to my house and sign the contract!

(BAPTISTA, MERCHANT, and TRANIO exit)

LUCENTIO: *(to audience)* There is an old priest waiting at the church to marry us right now. Bianca will be pleased. We're going to be together forever! Yippee!

(LUCENTIO exits)

ACT 4 SCENE 5

(enter PETRUCHIO, KATHERINA, HORTENSIO, and GRUMIO)

PETRUCHIO: What a great night for traveling to your dad's! How bright and goodly shines the moon!

KATHERINA: The moon? The sun! It's DAYTIME!

PETRUCHIO: I say it is the moon that shines so bright.

KATHERINA: I know it is the sun that shines so bright.

HORTENSIO: *(to KATHERINA)* Just say what he wants you to say, or we'll never get off this stage!

PETRUCHIO: I say it is the moon.

KATHERINA: *(looks at HORTENSIO and sighs loudly)* Fine. I know it is the moon.

PETRUCHIO: Then you lie. It is the blessed sun.

KATHERINA: Are you kidding me?! This is ridiculous! Okay, you win, it's the sun!

PETRUCHIO: That's what I like to hear! Let's get going! *(shoots a big happy grin to the audience)*

(enter VINCENTIO)

PETRUCHIO: A stranger! How exciting! Who are you, and where are you headed?

VINCENTIO: My name is Vincentio, and I'm traveling to see my son, Lucentio in Padua.

PETRUCHIO: Then we're family! Your son is marrying the sister to my wife, Kate. Her name's Bianca, and she's a super gal! Give me a hug! *(Gives VINCENTIO a big bear hug)*

VINCENTIO: Is this some sort of joke?

PETRUCHIO: Nope! Come on, we'll show you!

(ALL exit)

ACT 5 SCENE 1

(enter PETRUCHIO, KATHERINA, VINCENTIO, and GRUMIO)

PETRUCHIO: This is Lucentio's house.

VINCENTIO: *(yells loudly)* Hello? Anybody home?

(enter the MERCHANT, pretending to be VINCENTIO)

VINCENTIO: Hi. Is Lucentio within, sir?

MERCHANT: He's within, sir, but he's super busy. What's up?

VINCENTIO: I'm his dad, and I want to see him.

MERCHANT: Thou liest. I'M his dad. Not YOU.

VINCENTIO: What?! Who are you?!

(enter TRANIO pretending to be LUCENTIO and BAPTISTA)

TRANIO: *(to audience)* Uh-oh! The real Vincentio is here. This is getting fun!

VINCENTIO: Tranio!! What is going on?!

BAPTISTA: You mistake, sir. This is Lucentio.

TRANIO: Yeah, I'm Lucentio.

MERCHANT: Right! My son! I'm Vincentio...his FATHER.

VINCENTIO: This is nuts! Tell me, thou villain, where is my son Lucentio? The real one!

(enter LUCENTIO and BIANCA)

TRANIO: *(to MERCHANT)* Look guys, we better get the heck out of here! *(MERCHANT and TRANIO run offstage)*

LUCENTIO: *(to VINCENTIO)* Dad!! *(to BAPTISTA)* ...and Dad!

BAPTISTA and VINCENTIO: What?!

BIANCA: We got married. *(giggles)*

BAPTISTA: *(to LUCENTIO)* But you're Cambio, the poor teacher.

BIANCA: Cambio is changed into Lucentio! SO cool. I love him!

VINCENTIO: I need to sit down. Let's go inside and you can explain this all to me.

(everyone exits except KATHERINA and PETRUCHIO)

KATHERINA: Husband, let's follow to see what happens!

PETRUCHIO: First kiss me, Kate, and we will.

KATHERINA: Ew. Gross. No way.

PETRUCHIO: *(to audience)* Well, I tried. Come on!

(ALL exit)

ACT 5 SCENE 2

(enter LUCENTIO, PETRUCHIO, BAPTISTA, VINCENTIO, HORTENSIO, TRANIO, and GRUMIO)

LUCENTIO: What a great feast!

BAPTISTA: Both my lovely daughters are married! Although Petruchio, you did get stuck with the shrew!

PETRUCHIO: Well, I say no. She's really quite charming and agreeable.

HORTENSIO: Yeah, right. *(the men laugh)*

PETRUCHIO: Well, how about a challenge, then? Let's each one send unto his wife; and he whose wife comes right away, wins!

LUCENTIO: You're on! I bet a hundred crowns.

HORTENSIO: Me too!

PETRUCHIO: Fantastic. Who shall begin?

LUCENTIO: I will. Grumio – go and get Bianca.

(GRUMIO exits)

BAPTISTA: I'm sure Bianca will come right away!

(GRUMIO enters)

GRUMIO: Sorry, Lucentio, Bianca says that she is busy, and she cannot come.

(the men all groan and pat LUCENTIO on the back)

HORTENSIO: My turn! Grumio – go and get my wife.

(GRUMIO exits)

PETRUCHIO: Let's see how fast she'll come...

(GRUMIO enters)

GRUMIO: *(to HORTENSIO)* Your wife thinks this is a joke. She will not come. She bids you come to her.

(the men all groan and laugh and pat HORTENSIO on the back)

PETRUCHIO: My turn. Grumio – go and get my Kate!

(Grumio exits)

HORTENSIO: This will never happen.

(enter KATHERINA)

KATHERINA: Yes, dear?

(all the men have shocked looks on their faces)

PETRUCHIO: Where is your sister, and Hortensio's wife?

KATHERINA: Sitting by the parlor fire.

PETRUCHIO: Go and get them, please.

(KATHERINA exits)

LUCENTIO and HORTENSIO: Whooooooa.

BAPTISTA: Petruchio wins the bet! Now, what have you done with my daughter? That couldn't be my Katherina!

(enter KATHERINA, BIANCA, and the WIDOW)

WIDOW: What in the world do you men want now?

PETRUCHIO: Kate, please explain to these headstrong women how to be good wives.

WIDOW: You've GOT to be kidding me.

KATHERINA: *(to BIANCA and the WIDOW, with a wink and a smile)* No, I've got this. *(to everyone)* Ahem! Thy husband is thy lord, thy life, thy keeper, and we ladies should be nice and LOVE him. *(to PETRUCHIO)* How'd I do?

PETRUCHIO: Couldn't have said it better myself. Come on, wonderful wife, let's go to sleep. Good-night everybody!

(PETRUCHIO and KATHERINA exit)

HORTENSIO: I can't believe he tamed a curst shrew!

LUCENTIO: Totally unbelievable, but true!

(ALL exit)

THE END

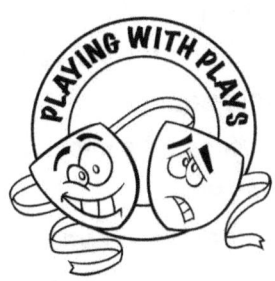

The 25-Minute or so Taming of the Shrew

By William Shakespeare

Creatively modified by

Khara C. Barnhart and Brendan P. Kelso

14-19+ Actors

CAST OF CHARACTERS:

KATHERINA: the SHREW (she's not very nice)

BIANCA: Katherina's younger, super cute sister

[1]**BAPTISTA:** Katherina and Bianca's father

PETRUCHIO: trying to tame the Shrew (Katherina)

[2]**GREMIO:** old rich dude who wants to marry Bianca

GRUMIO: Petruchio's servant (who puts a Gremio AND a Grumio in the same play?!)

[3]**LUCENTIO:** loves Bianca and pretends to be a teacher named Cambio

HORTENSIO: loves Bianca and pretends to be a musician named Litio

TRANIO: Lucentio's servant who pretends to be Lucentio (confused yet?)

BIONDELLO: Lucentio's other servant

VINCENTIO: Lucentio's dad

[4]**MERCHANT:** pretends to be Lucentio's dad

WIDOW: a rich widow

[2]**CURTIS:** one of Petruchio's servants

[1]**NATHANIEL:** another one of Petruchio's servants

[3]**JOSEPH:** yet another one of Petruchio's servants

[4]**PHILIP:** you guessed it...one of Petruchio's many servants

NICHOLAS: and the last of Petruchio's servants!

[4]**SERVANT:** because we need more servants
TOWNSFOLK: they live in the town

The same actors can play the following parts:
[1]BAPTISTA and NATHANIEL
[2]GREMIO and CURTIS
[3]LUCENTIO and JOSEPH
[4]MERCHANT, PHILIP, and the SERVANT
TOWNSFOLK can be extras as needed

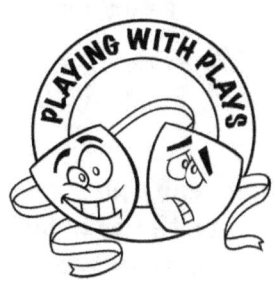

ACT 1 SCENE 1

(enter LUCENTIO and TRANIO)

LUCENTIO: Well, Tranio, my trusty servant, here we are in Padua, Italy! I can't wait to start studying and learn all about philosophy and virtue!

TRANIO: There is such a thing as too much studying, master Lucentio. We need to remember to have fun too! PARTY!

LUCENTIO: Hey look! Here come some of the locals!

(LUCENTIO and TRANIO move to side of stage; Enter BAPTISTA, KATHERINA, BIANCA, HORTENSIO, and GREMIO)

BAPTISTA: Look guys, you know the rules: Bianca can't marry anybody until her older sister, Katherina, is married. That's the plan and I'm sticking to it! If either of you both love Katherina, then please, take her.

KATHERINA: *(Sarcastically)* Wow, thanks, Dad.

HORTENSIO: I wouldn't marry her if she were the last woman on earth.

KATHERINA: And I'd rather scratch your face off than marry you!

TRANIO: *(aside to LUCENTIO)* That wench is stark mad!

BAPTISTA: Enough of this! Bianca, go inside.

BIANCA: Yes, dearest father. My books and instruments shall be my company. *(she exits)*

KATHERINA: *(At BIANCA)* Goody two-shoes.

BAPTISTA: Bianca is so talented in music, instruments, and poetry! I really need to hire some tutors for her. *(KATHERINA rolls her eyes and sighs)* Good-day everyone! *(BAPTISTA exits)*

KATHERINA: *(Very angry)* AGHHHH!!!! I'm outta here *(exits opposite direction from her father)*

GREMIO: *(Shudders)* Ugh! How could anyone ever want to marry Katherina?!

HORTENSIO: I don't know, but let's find a husband for her.

GREMIO: A husband? A devil!

HORTENSIO: I say a husband.

GREMIO: I say a devil.

HORTENSIO: Alright, alright! There's got to be a guy out there crazy enough to marry her.

GREMIO: Let's get to it!

(exit GREMIO and HORTENSIO)

LUCENTIO: Oh, Tranio! Sweet Bianca, has stolen my heart! I burn, I pine, I perish! Oh, how I love her!

TRANIO: Whoa, Master! You're getting a little overdramatic, there, Lucentio.

LUCENTIO: Sorry. But my heart is seriously on fire! How am I going to make her fall in love with me if she's not allowed to date anybody? Hmmm...

TRANIO: What if you pretended to be a tutor and went to teach her?

LUCENTIO: YOU ARE BRILLIANT, TRANIO! And because we're new here and no one knows what we look like yet, YOU will pretend to be ME at all the local parties. Quick, let's change clothes.

TRANIO: Here? Now? *(points at audience)* In front of my parents?

LUCENTIO: Yes, Here and now! You can't stop this lovin' feeling! *(starts singing a love song)*

TRANIO: Please, no singing. I'll do it. *(they exchange hats, socks or jackets)*

LUCENTIO: Perfect! Now while you're pretending to be me, try and get Bianca to marry you. I've got a super confusing plan that I'll tell you about later. Got it?

TRANIO: Huh? I am already confused. But, yeah, got it.

(ALL exit)

ACT 1 SCENE 2

(enter PETRUCHIO and GRUMIO; HORTENSIO enters from opposite side of stage)

HORTENSIO: Petruchio and Grumio! What happy gale blows you to Padua here from old Verona?

PETRUCHIO: Such wind as scatters young men through the world.

GRUMIO: Why don't you tell him why you're REALLY here, Petruchio.

PETRUCHIO: OK, fine. I'm here to find a rich wife. And I mean, RICH!

HORTENSIO: Listen, Petruchio, I know a girl who is very rich, but who is also shrewd and ill-favored. Really, she's just MEAN.

PETRUCHIO: Hortensio, I don't care if she's mean, old, smelly AND ugly. If she's rich, that's all that matters! I come to wive it wealthily in Padua!

GRUMIO: Who is she?

HORTENSIO: Her name is Katherina, renowned in Padua for her scolding tongue.

PETRUCHIO: She sounds awesome! I will not sleep, Hortensio, till I see her. Can we go now?

HORTENSIO: *(to audience)* This is great! I'll take him, but I will disguise myself as a music teacher. That way I can teach Bianca and get her to fall in love with me!

(enter GREMIO and LUCENTIO, disguised as a teacher, CAMBIO)

HORTENSIO: *(to PETRUCHIO and GRUMIO)* Ah, look! That's Gremio. He also wants to marry Bianca, but he doesn't have a chance against me!

(HORTENSIO walks over to GREMIO and LUCENTIO)

HORTENSIO: Hey there, old man! I have some good news! I may have found a husband for Katherina *(points to PETRUCHIO)*...which means Bianca would be fair game.

GREMIO: Have you told him all her faults? *(to PETRUCHIO)* Will you woo this wildcat?

PETRUCHIO: Come on, guys, she can't be that bad. So she has a bad temper. I can deal with it. I am very brave. *(Starts posing like a hero or a bodybuilder; Enter TRANIO pretending to be LUCENTIO)*

TRANIO: Hello gentlemen! Do any of you know the way to Signor Baptista's house? I heard he has a beautiful daughter.

PETRUCHIO: You're not talking about the mean one, right?

TRANIO: Mean? No, no, no... I want the nice one. Bianca.

GREMIO: Sorry, new guy, but Bianca's mine.

HORTENSIO: Not exactly, Gremio, she's actually mine.

TRANIO: Let's just consider her mine, okay?

LUCENTIO: *(to TRANIO, whispering)* You are doing a great job at pretending to be me! Keep it up!

PETRUCHIO: Remember guys, nobody can have Bianca until the elder sister first be wed.

(ALL exit)

ACT 2 SCENE 1

(enter KATHERINA and BIANCA, hands tied)

BIANCA: Katherina, you can't treat me like a slave. Unbind my hands, and I'll give you anything you want!

KATHERINA: I want to know which man you love the most.

BIANCA: I don't like any of them.

KATHERINA: Thou liest. What about Hortensio?

BIANCA: No... if you want him, you shall have him.

KATHERINA: Ew! No thanks. So you like old rich guys like Gremio, then?

BIANCA: You must be joking. Sister Kate, untie my hands.

(KATHERINA sticks out her tongue at BIANCA, who starts crying; Enter BAPTISTA)

BAPTISTA: Girls! Stop this! *(to KATHERINA)* For shame... what the!? ...What did your sister ever do to you? *(BIANCA exits)*

KATHERINA: You always take her side! She is your treasure, she must have a husband, I must dance barefoot on her wedding day. Just leave me alone. I will go sit and weep and think of a way to get my revenge! *(KATHERINA exits)*

(enter GREMIO, LUCENTIO disguised as CAMBIO, PETRUCHIO, HORTENSIO disguised as LITIO, and TRANIO disguised as LUCENTIO)

BAPTISTA: Hello gentlemen.

PETRUCHIO: Have you not a daughter called Katherina, fair and virtuous?

BAPTISTA: I have a daughter, sir....called Katherina.

PETRUCHIO: Perfect! I have brought my friend, Litio *(PETRUCHIO pushes HORTENSIO forward towards BAPTISTA)*, who's a totally rockin' musician. I think he'd be an excellent teacher for her.

BAPTISTA: Yeah, sounds great, but Katherina is... well... difficult.

GREMIO: *(to audience)* You can say that again! *(to BAPTISTA)* Baptista, may I present Cambio *(he pushes LUCENTIO towards BAPTISTA)*, a young scholar, who is super duper smart. He'd make a great teacher for Bianca.

BAPTISTA: This is wonderful. Welcome to our household Litio and Cambio. Go on inside! *(HORTENSIO and LUCENTIO exit)*

BAPTISTA: *(to TRANIO)* And who might you be?

TRANIO: I'm Lucentio. I think your daughter Bianca is amazing, and I want to date her!

BAPTISTA: Well, the more, the merrier.

PETRUCHIO: Signor Baptista, I'm in a rush to get married.

BAPTISTA: Okay, if you can get Katherina to love you, you can have her.

PETRUCHIO: I'm a pretty macho guy, Baptista. I'll get her to love me, no problemo.

(enter HORTENSIO disguised as LITIO, stumbling and holding a broken guitar)

BAPTISTA: Why dost thou look so pale? Will my daughter make a good musician?

HORTENSIO: I think she'll sooner prove a soldier! She broke the guitar over my head and called me terrible names!

PETRUCHIO: Sweet! I can't wait to meet this terror of a girl!

BAPTISTA: *(to HORTENSIO)* Go ahead and teach my younger daughter instead. She's much nicer. Petruchio, you stay here and I'll send Katherina out. *(ALL exit except for PETRUCHIO)*

PETRUCHIO: *(to Audience)* This ought to be good!!

(enter KATHERINA)

PETRUCHIO: Good morrow Kate; for that's your name, I hear. Kate...Kate...Kate!

KATHERINA: It's Katherina.

PETRUCHIO: You lie, in faith, for you are called plain Kate, and bonny Kate, and sometimes Kate the curst... but you are my super-dainty Kate, and I am going to marry you.

KATHERINA: *(Starts laughing hysterically)* Riiiiiiiiiiiiiiiiight. And I'm the queen of England.

PETRUCHIO: Oh, come on, sweet Kitty "Kat." Here.... kitty, kitty, kitty...

KATHERINA: Hiss!!

PETRUCHIO: Come, come, you wasp. I'faith, you are too angry.

KATHERINA: If I be waspish, best beware my sting! *(she swings at PETRUCHIO)*

PETRUCHIO: Okay, I get it. No more animal references. But you will be my wife; I am born to tame you, Kate!

(enter BAPTISTA, GREMIO and TRANIO disguised as LUCENTIO)

BAPTISTA: So, how'd it go?

PETRUCHIO: Great!

KATHERINA: Terrible!

PETRUCHIO: *(Holds hand over KATHERINA'S mouth so she can't talk)* We've decided that Sunday is the wedding day.

BAPTISTA: Wonderful! I'll start the preparations.

PETRUCHIO: And I'll go buy fancy clothes and rings. *(KATHERINA elbows PETRUCHIO in the side)* Woo-hoo! *(PETRUCHIO exits one direction, while KATHERINA storms off stage in the opposite direction)*

TRANIO: Alright! Now we can finally talk about Bianca! I love her so!

GREMIO: I saw her first!! Thou canst not love so dear as I.

TRANIO: Yes I CANST!

BAPTISTA: Look, it's simple: whoever has the most money gets Bianca.

GREMIO: I have tons of money. *(Starts throwing dollars all over the stage and in the audience)*

TRANIO: I have more! *(Pulls out his credit card)*

BAPTISTA: *(Grabs credit card)* Okay then, Lucentio, you get Bianca! You can marry her after Katherina's wedding, IF you can get your father to pay the dowry. If not, then Gremio can have her. *(BAPTISTA exits)*

GREMIO: Good luck, daddy's boy! *(exits)*

TRANIO: *(to audience)* I'd say I've been doing a pretty good job pretending to be Lucentio. But now I have to find someone to pretend to be my dad... I mean Lucentio's dad!

(TRANIO exits)

ACT 3 SCENE 1

(enter HORTENSIO disguised as LITIO, LUCENTIO disguised as CAMBIO and BIANCA)

LUCENTIO: Ok, Bianca, let's hit the books! I have so much to teach you today!

HORTENSIO: I don't think so, Cambio. Music first, then you can get to your boring books...SNORE!

BIANCA: Let me choose; I'll learn my lessons as I please myself. Books first.

(LUCENTIO pumps his fist in the air as a "winner," while HORTENSIO walks to the side of the stage and pouts)

LUCENTIO: *(Opens a large book)* THIS, sweet Bianca, is Latin.

BIANCA: Got it. Next? *(she turns to HORTENSIO)* What'cha got, Litio?

HORTENSIO: THIS, dear Bianca, is Rock and Roll. *(begins playing on his guitar like a rock musician and gets carried away)*

BIANCA: Got it.

(enter SERVANT)

SERVANT: Mistress, your father prays you leave your books and come help your sister get ready for her wedding tomorrow.

BIANCA: Farewell, sweet masters both. I must be gone. *(BIANCA and SERVANT exit)*

HORTENSIO and LUCENTIO: Bye Bianca!

(they give each other dirty looks and exit opposite sides of the stage)

ACT 3 SCENE 2

(enter BAPTISTA, GREMIO, TRANIO disguised as LUCENTIO, KATHERINA, BIANCA, and LUCENTIO disguised as CAMBIO)

BAPTISTA: *(to TRANIO)* Oh, Lucentio, today's the day that Katherine and Petruchio should be married, but Petruchio is nowhere to be found!

KATHERINA: I told you, he was a frantic fool!

TRANIO: Patience, good Katherine, and Baptista too. He'll be here, don't worry!

KATHERINA: What-EVER! *(she exits and Bianca follows her offstage)*

(enter BIONDELLO)

BIONDELLO: You guys will never believe this! Petruchio is coming, but he looks ridiculous!

BAPTISTA: What do you mean?

BIONDELLO: Well, his pants are inside out, his boots are mismatched and falling apart, and he's got an old rusty sword! Oh, but he's got a new hat! Look! *(PETRUCHIO enters looking like a clown, with GRUMIO).*

PETRUCHIO: Who's ready for a wedding?! *(looks around)* But where is Kate? Where is my love?

BAPTISTA: You know this is your wedding day...right? You will not marry her looking like that!

PETRUCHIO: Oh yes I will! Better get to the church! *(PETRUCHIO and GRUMIO exit)*

BAPTISTA: I better go too. Come on, Gremio! *(BAPTISTA and GREMIO exit)*

TRANIO: *(to LUCENTIO)* Good news, Lucentio! Baptista said I –er... YOU could marry Bianca, as long as your father can provide the money. I will get a man to pretend to be your dad, Vincentio, so you can marry sweet Bianca right away!

LUCENTIO: Awesome plan!

(enter GREMIO)

GREMIO: That was the weirdest wedding I've ever been to! Petruchio yelled like a crazy man, knocked down the priest, and scared everyone half to death! I've never seen anything like it!

LUCENTIO: Here they come!

(enter PETRUCHIO, KATHERINA, BIANCA, BAPTISTA, HORTENSIO, GRUMIO and TOWNSFOLK)

PETRUCHIO: Friends, I thank you for showing up, but now we must go. Come on, Kate!

KATHERINA: But I'm hungry and there's this huge feast waiting! Now, if you love me, stay.

PETRUCHIO: We're leaving!

KATHERINA: Oh, you mean...terrible...rotten worm!

PETRUCHIO: *(mocking her)* I know you are but what am I?

KATHERINA: Stop it!

PETRUCHIO: Fine! *(to everyone else onstage)* You all go party, be mad and merry. Kate belongs to me now, and I'm taking her home. *(PETRUCHIO grabs KATHERINA and exits, followed by GRUMIO; KATHERINA screams until they are offstage; everyone onstage is shocked and silent)*

LUCENTIO: *(to BIANCA)* Mistress, what's your opinion of your sister?

BIANCA: That being mad herself, she's madly mated.

BAPTISTA: Well, let's not waste the wedding food! Come, gentlemen, let's go eat!

(ALL exit)

ACT 4 SCENE 1

(enter GRUMIO and CURTIS)

CURTIS: Is my master, Petruchio, and his wife coming, Grumio?

GRUMIO: They'll be here any second. We're all tired and hungry. Hey, call the other servants.

CURTIS *(Calls offstage)* Yo! Get in here, now!

(enter NATHANIEL, PHILIP, JOSEPH, and NICHOLAS)

NATHANIEL: Welcome home, Grumio.

PHILIP: How now, Grumio?

JOSEPH: What, Grumio!

NICHOLAS: Fellow Grumio!

GRUMIO: Hey there fellows!

(enter PETRUCHIO and KATHERINA)

PETRUCHIO: Where be these knaves? Where are my servants?

ALL SERVANTS: Here, here, sir!

PETRUCHIO: *(mockingly)* "Here, sir. Here sir!" You loggerheaded and unpolished grooms! Go rascals, go and fetch my supper. NOW!

(ALL SERVANTS exit)

PETRUCHIO: Sit down, Kate, and welcome. *(Starts sniffing the air and then yells off stage)* You villains burned the meat! I can smell it from here! Yuck! Throw it away! You heedless joltheads and unmannered slaves!

KATHERINA: It smells fine to me...and I'm so hungry!

PETRUCHIO: I tell thee, Kate, 'twas burnt and dried away. No dinner for us tonight. Come on, let's go to bed. *(they exit together then PETRUCHIO reenters alone)*

PETRUCHIO: *(to audience)* This is the "taming" part of the "Taming of the Shrew." Get it? She ate no meat today, nor none will eat. Last night she slept not, nor to-night she shall not. I'm going to make her miserable until she becomes a better person. This will be so fun!

(PETRUCHIO exits)

(enter TRANIO disguised as LUCENTIO and HORTENSIO disguised as LITIO)

TRANIO: I think that Bianca is totally in love with me, don't you?

HORTENSIO: Ha! You think so, Lucentio? Just watch....

(enter BIANCA and LUCENTIO disguised as CAMBIO)

BIANCA: *(to LUCENTIO)* What are we going to study today?

LUCENTIO: My favorite book: The Art to Love!

BIANCA: Sweet! I love love!

LUCENTIO: And I love you!

HORTENSIO: *(to TRANIO)* Now, tell me, I pray, what were you saying about Bianca being in love with you?

TRANIO: Aghhh...O despiteful love! Guess I was wrong.

HORTENSIO: Okay, listen. I am not Litio, nor a musician. My real name is Hortensio.

TRANIO: Well, Hortensio, it looks like Bianca loves that Cambio guy. Should we give up?

HORTENSIO: Yep! I'm going to marry a wealthy widow in town. And so farewell. *(HORTENSIO exits)*

TRANIO: Hey lovebirds! Hortensio's off to go to marry some rich widow.

BIANCA: God give him joy!

LUCENTIO: *(to BIANCA)* Now you're all mine!

BIANCA: Oh, Cambio! I mean...Lucentio. *(giggles)* I'm still getting used to all this "disguise" stuff.

(enter BIONDELLO)

BIONDELLO: I think I found an old guy to pretend to be your dad! He's coming this way now.

LUCENTIO: Cool!

TRANIO: You guys get out of here and leave this to me!

(LUCENTIO, BIANCA, and BIONDELLO exit)(enter the MERCHANT)

TRANIO: Hello there! What brings you to Padua?

MERCHANT: Just passing through on business.

TRANIO: *(overly dramatic)* You know, it can be dangerous in this part of the world... but, if you pretend to be my father, Vincentio, you can stay at my house while you're here and I'll keep you safe. How does that sound?

MERCHANT: Sounds like a plan!

TRANIO: Perfect.

(ALL exit)

ACT 4 SCENE 3

(enter KATHERINA and GRUMIO)

KATHERINA: Please, please, please? Won't you give me any food? I am SOOOOO hungry!

GRUMIO: I dare not for my life.

(enter PETRUCHIO and HORTENSIO)

KATHERINA: But I'm starving!! If you don't feed me, I'll die!

PETRUCHIO: Oh, don't be so dramatic! This isn't Romeo and Juliet – no one's dying in this play.

HORTENSIO: *(to PETRUCHIO)* Shouldn't you feed her? Aren't you going too far in this "taming" business?

PETRUCHIO: Don't you worry about it! O Grumio, Grumio! Wherefore art thou, Grumio?

GRUMIO: Uh, I'm right here, Petruchio.

PETRUCHIO: Did the new cap and gown I ordered for sweet Kate arrive? *(Gives an evil grin to the audience)*

GRUMIO: Yes, come with me, and I'll show you.

(exit PETRUCHIO, KATHERINA, and GRUMIO)

HORTENSIO: *(to Audience)* I've got a bad feeling about this.

(enter PETRUCHIO, KATHERINA, and GRUMIO)

PETRUCHIO: That hat was way too small for your big head. It's like a toy or a baby's cap. Throw it out!

KATHERINA: I like the cap, and I will have it.

PETRUCHIO: When you are gentle, you shall have one.

KATHERINA: I am no child. Quit treating me like a baby!!

PETRUCHIO: Then quit whining like a baby! You know what? That dress was really ugly. *(to GRUMIO)* Throw that out too!

KATHERINA: Are you nuts! I never saw a better-fashioned gown.

PETRUCHIO: Sorry, Kate. We'll head back to your father's house in our plain old, dirty clothes. In fact, we'll not go today. We'll go see your dad tomorrow.

KATHERINA: Aghhhhhhhhhhhhhhhhh! I am sooooo mad!!!!!!! *(Starts stomping her feet; PETRUCHIO, KATHERINA, and GRUMIO exit)*

HORTENSIO: *(to Audience)* Who does he think he is, the king? I'm glad I don't live here!

(HORTENSIO exits)

ACT 4 SCENE 4

(enter TRANIO disguised as LUCENTIO and the MERCHANT disguised as VINCENTIO)

TRANIO: Ready?

MERCHANT: Yes I am...son! From now on, I am your father whose name is Vincentio.

(enter BIONDELLO)

TRANIO: Hey there, Biondello, this guy is pretending to be my father, so just go along with it, got it?

BIONDELLO: Got it!

(enter BAPTISTA and LUCENTIO disguised as CAMBIO)

MERCHANT: Good day, Baptista! My son tells me he's in love with your daughter, Bianca, and wants to marry her. I am content to let the wedding happen.

BAPTISTA: Thanks! If you can show me the money, then the match is made and all is done. Your son shall have my daughter with consent.

TRANIO: Let's go back to my house and sign the contract!

(BAPTISTA, MERCHANT, and TRANIO exit)

BIONDELLO: Okay, Cambio or Lucentio or whatever your name is now... If you want to go marry Bianca, the old priest is waiting for you at the church right now. *(BIONDELLO exits)*

LUCENTIO: Oh, my happy heart! Bianca will be pleased. We're going to be together forever! Yippee!

(LUCENTIO exits)

(enter PETRUCHIO, KATHERINA, HORTENSIO, and SERVANTS)

PETRUCHIO: What a great night for traveling to your dad's! How bright and goodly shines the moon!

KATHERINA: The moon? The sun! It's DAYTIME!

PETRUCHIO: I say it is the moon that shines so bright.

KATHERINA: I know it is the sun that shines so bright.

HORTENSIO: *(to KATHERINA)* Just say what he wants you to say, or we'll never get off this stage!

PETRUCHIO: I say it is the moon.

KATHERINA: *(looks at HORTENSIO and sighs loudly)* Fine. I know it is the moon.

PETRUCHIO: Then you lie. It is the blessed sun.

KATHERINA: Are you kidding me?! This is ridiculous! Okay, you win, it's the sun!

PETRUCHIO: That's what I like to hear! Let's get going! *(shoots a big happy grin to the audience; Enter VINCENTIO)*

PETRUCHIO: A stranger! How exciting! Who are you, and where are you headed?

VINCENTIO: My name is Vincentio, and I'm traveling to see my son, Lucentio in Padua.

PETRUCHIO: Then we're family! Your son is marrying the sister to my wife, Kate. Her name's Bianca, and she's a super gal! Give me a hug! *(Gives VINCENTIO a big bear hug)*

VINCENTIO: Is this some sort of joke?

PETRUCHIO: Nope! Come on, we'll show you!

(ALL exit)

ACT 5 SCENE 1

(enter GREMIO, PETRUCHIO, KATHERINA, VINCENTIO, and GRUMIO)

PETRUCHIO: This is Lucentio's house.

VINCENTIO: *(yells loudly)* Hello? Anybody home?

(enter the MERCHANT, pretending to be VINCENTIO)

VINCENTIO: Hi. Is Lucentio within, sir?

MERCHANT: He's within, sir, but he's super busy. What's up?

VINCENTIO: I'm his dad, and I want to see him.

MERCHANT: Thou liest. I'M his dad. Not YOU.

VINCENTIO: What?! Who are you?!

(enter BIONDELLO)

BIONDELLO: *(to audience)* Uh-oh! The real Vincentio is here. This is getting fun!

VINCENTIO: *(to BIONDELLO)* Come hither, you rogue! What, have you forgot me?

BIONDELLO: No sir. I could never forget you, for I never saw you before in all my life! *(Winks at audience)*

VINCENTIO: What, you notorious villain, I'm Lucentio's dad and you are his servant! *(Starts chasing BIONDELLO around the stage, trying to hit him, but missing over and over)*

BIONDELLO: Help, help, help! Here's a madman will murder me! *(he runs offstage; VINCENTIO is left looking VERY frustrated and confused; Enter TRANIO pretending to be LUCENTIO and BAPTISTA)*

VINCENTIO: Tranio!! What is going on?!

BAPTISTA: You mistake, sir. This is Lucentio.

TRANIO: Yeah, I'm Lucentio.

MERCHANT: Right! My son! I'm Vincentio...his FATHER.

VINCENTIO: This is nuts! Tell me, thou villain, where is my son Lucentio? The real one!

GREMIO: *(moans)* I'm too old for this.

(enter BIONDELLO, LUCENTIO, and BIANCA)

BIONDELLO: *(to the MERCHANT and TRANIO)* Look guys, we better get the heck out of here! *(BIONDELLO, MERCHANT, and TRANIO run offstage)*

LUCENTIO: *(to VINCENTIO)* Dad!! *(to BAPTISTA)* ...and Dad!

BAPTISTA and VINCENTIO: What?!

BIANCA: We got married. *(giggles)*

BAPTISTA: *(to LUCENTIO)* But you're Cambio, the poor teacher.

BIANCA: Cambio is changed into Lucentio! SO cool. I love him!

VINCENTIO: I need to sit down. Let's go inside and you can explain this all to me.

(everyone exits except KATHERINA and PETRUCHIO)

KATHERINA: Husband, let's follow to see what happens!

PETRUCHIO: First kiss me, Kate, and we will.

KATHERINA: Ew. Gross. No way.

PETRUCHIO: Well, I tried. Come on!

(ALL exit)

ACT 5 SCENE 2

(enter LUCENTIO, PETRUCHIO, BAPTISTA, VINCENTIO, GREMIO, the MERCHANT, HORTENSIO, TRANIO, BIONDELLO, and GRUMIO)

LUCENTIO: What a great feast!

BAPTISTA: Both my lovely daughters are married! Although Petruchio, you did get stuck with the shrew!

PETRUCHIO: Well, I say no. She's really quite charming and agreeable.

HORTENSIO: Yeah, right. (the men laugh)

PETRUCHIO: Well, how about a challenge, then? Let's each one send unto his wife; and he whose wife comes right away, wins!

LUCENTIO: You're on! I bet a hundred crowns.

HORTENSIO: Me too!

PETRUCHIO: Fantastic. Who shall begin?

LUCENTIO: I will. Biondello – go and get Bianca.

(BIONDELLO exits)

BAPTISTA: I'm sure Bianca will come right away!

(BIONDELLO enters)

BIONDELLO: Sorry, Lucentio, Bianca says that she is busy, and she cannot come.

(the men all groan and pat LUCENTIO on the back)

GREMIO: At least she was nice about it! I can just imagine what Katherina will say when it's her turn!

PETRUCHIO: Oh, just wait...

HORTENSIO: My turn! Biondello – go and get my wife.

(BIONDELLO exits)

PETRUCHIO: Let's see how fast she'll come...

(BIONDELLO enters)

BIONDELLO: *(to HORTENSIO)* Your wife thinks this is a joke. She will not come. She bids you come to her.

(the men all groan and laugh and pat HORTENSIO on the back)

PETRUCHIO: My turn. Grumio – go and get my Kate!

(Grumio exits)

HORTENSIO: This will never happen.

(enter KATHERINA)

KATHERINA: Yes, dear?

(all the men have shocked looks on their faces)

PETRUCHIO: Where is your sister, and Hortensio's wife?

KATHERINA: Sitting by the parlor fire.

PETRUCHIO: Go and get them, please.

(KATHERINA exits)

LUCENTIO and HORTENSIO: Whoooooooa.

BAPTISTA: Petruchio wins the bet! Now, what have you done with my daughter? That couldn't be my Katherina!

(enter KATHERINA, BIANCA, and the WIDOW)

WIDOW: What in the world do you men want now?

PETRUCHIO: Kate, please explain to these headstrong women how to be good wives.

WIDOW: You've GOT to be kidding me.

KATHERINA: *(to BIANCA and the WIDOW, with a wink and a smile)* No, I've got this. *(to everyone)* Ahem! Thy husband is thy lord, thy life, thy keeper, and we ladies should be nice and LOVE him. *(to PETRUCHIO)* How'd I do?

PETRUCHIO: Couldn't have said it better myself. Come on, wonderful wife, let's go to sleep. Good-night everybody!

(PETRUCHIO and KATHERINA exit)

HORTENSIO: I can't believe he tamed a curst shrew!

LUCENTIO: Totally unbelievable, but true!

(ALL exit)

THE END

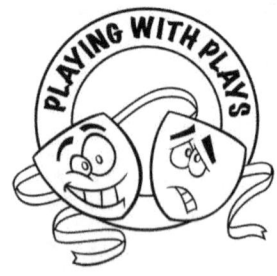

Sneak Peeks at other Playing With Plays books:

King Lear for Kids

ACT 1 SCENE 1

KING LEAR's palace

(enter FOOL entertaining the audience with jokes, dancing, juggling, Hula Hooping... whatever the actor's skill may be; enter KENT)

KENT: Hey, Fool!

FOOL: What did you call me?!

KENT: I called you Fool.

FOOL: That's my name, don't wear it out! *(to audience)* Seriously, that's my name in the play!

(enter LEAR, CORNWALL, ALBANY, GONERIL, REGAN, and CORDELIA)

LEAR: The lords of France and Burgundy are outside. They both want to marry you, Cordelia.

ALL: Ooooooo!

LEAR: *(to audience)* Between you and me she IS my favorite child! *(to the girls)* Daughters, I need to talk to you about something. It's a really big deal.

GONERIL & REGAN: Did you buy us presents?

LEAR: This is even better than presents!

GONERIL & REGAN: Goody, goody!!!

CORDELIA: Father, your love is enough for me.

LEAR: Give me the map there, Kent. Girls, I'm tired. I've made a decision: Know that we - and by 'we' I mean 'me' - have divided in three our kingdom...

KENT: Whoa! Sir, dividing the kingdom may cause chaos! People could die!

FOOL: Well, this IS a tragedy...

LEAR: You worry too much, Kent. I'm giving it to my daughters so their husbands can be rich and powerful... like me!

CORNWALL & ALBANY: Sweet!

GONERIL & REGAN: Wait... what?

CORDELIA: This is olden times. That means that everything we own belongs to our husbands.

GONERIL & REGAN: Olden times stink!

CORDELIA: Truth.

LEAR: So, my daughters, tell your daddy how much you love him. Goneril, our eldest-born, speak first.

GONERIL: Sir, I love you more than words can say! More than outer space, puppies and cotton candy! I love you more than any child has ever loved a father in the history of the entire world, dearest Pops!

CORDELIA: *(to audience)* Holy moly! Surely, he won't be fooled by that. *(to self)* Love, and be silent.

LEAR: Thanks, sweetie! I'm giving you this big chunk of the kingdom here. What says our second daughter, Our dearest Regan, wife to Cornwall? Speak.

REGAN: What she said, Daddy... times a thousand!

CORDELIA: *(to audience)* What?! I love my father more than either of them. But I can't express it in words. My love's more richer than my tongue.

LEAR: Wow, Regan! You get this big hunk of the kingdom. Cordelia, what can you tell me to get this giant piece of kingdom as your own? Speak.

CORDELIA: Nothing, my lord.

LEAR: Nothing?!?

CORDELIA: Nothing.

LEAR: Come on, now. Nothing will come of nothing.

CORDELIA: I love you as a daughter loves her father.

LEAR: Try a little, harder, sweetie!

CORDELIA: Why are my sisters married if they give you all their love?

LEAR: How did you get so mean?

CORDELIA: Father, I will not insult you by telling you my love is like... as big as a whale.

LEAR: *(getting mad)* Fine. I'll split your share between your sisters.

REGAN, GONERIL, & CORNWALL: Yessss!

KENT: Whoa! Let's all just calm down a minute!

LEAR: Peace, Kent! You don't want to mess with me right now. I told you she was my favorite...

GONERIL & REGAN: What!?

LEAR: ...and she can't even tell me she loves me more than a whale? Nope. Now I'm mad.

KENT: Royal Lear, really...

LEAR: Kent, I'm pretty emotional right now! You better not try to talk me out of this...

KENT: Sir, you're acting ... insane.

The Three Musketeers for Kids

(ATHOS and D'ARTAGNAN enter)

ATHOS: Glad you could make it. I have engaged two of my friends as seconds.

D'ARTAGNAN: Seconds?

ATHOS: Yeah, they make sure we fight fair. Oh, here they are now!

(enter ARAMIS and PORTHOS singing, "Bad boys, bad boys, watcha gonna do...")

PORTHOS: Hey! I'm fighting him in an hour. I am going to fight... because...well... I am going to fight!

ARAMIS: And I fight him at two o'clock! Ours is a theological quarrel. *(does a thinking pose)*

D'ARTAGNAN: Yeah, yeah, yeah... I'll get to you soon!

ATHOS: We are the Three Musketeers; Athos, Porthos, and Aramis.

D'ARTAGNAN: Whatever, Ethos, Pathos, and Logos, let's just finish this! *(swords crossed and are about to fight; enter JUSSAC and cardinal's guards)*

PORTHOS: The cardinal's guards! Sheathe your swords, gentlemen.

JUSSAC: Dueling is illegal! You are under arrest!

ARAMIS: *(to ATHOS and PORTHOS)* There are five of them and we are but three.

D'ARTAGNAN: *(steps forward to join them)* It appears to me we are four! I have the spirit; my heart is that of a Musketeer.

PORTHOS: Great! I love fighting!

(Musketeers say "Fight, fight fight!...Fight, fight, fight!" as they are fighting; D'ARTAGNAN fights JUSSAC and it's the big fight; JUSSAC is wounded and exits; the 3 MUSKETEERS cheer)

ATHOS: Well done! Let's go see Treville and the king!

ARAMIS: And we don't have to kill you now!

PORTHOS: And let's get some food, too! I'm hungry!

D'ARTAGNAN: *(to audience)* This is fun!

(ALL exit)

ACT 2 SCENE 1

(enter 3 MUSKETEERS, D'ARTAGNAN, and TREVILLE)

TREVILLE: The king wants to see you, and he's not too happy you killed a few of the cardinal's guards.

(enter KING)

KING: *(yelling)* YOU GUYS HUMILIATED THE CARDINAL'S GUARDS!

ATHOS: Sire, they attacked us!

KING: Oh...Well then, bravo! I hear D'Artagnan beat the cardinal's best swordsman! Brave young man! Here's some money for you. Enjoy! *(hands money to D'ARTAGNAN)*

D'ARTAGNAN: Sweet!

(ALL exit)

Sneak peek of
Oliver Twist
for Kids

(enter FAGIN, SIKES, DODGER and NANCY)

DODGER: So that Oliver kid got caught by the police.

FAGIN: He could tell them all our secrets and get us in trouble; we've got to find him. Like, in the next 30 seconds or so.

SIKES: Send Nancy. She's good at getting information quick.

NANCY: Nope. Don't wanna go, Sikes. I like the kid.

SIKES: She'll go, Fagin.

NANCY: No, she won't, Fagin.

SIKES: Yes, she will, Fagin.

NANCY: Fine! Grrrrr....

(NANCY sticks out her tongue at SIKES and storms offstage, then immediately returns)

NANCY: Okay, I checked with my sources and, some gentleman took him home to take care of him.

(NANCY, DODGER and SIKES stare at FAGIN waiting for direction)

FAGIN: Where?

NANCY: I don't know.

FAGIN: WHAT!?!? *(waiting)* Well don't just stand there, GO FIND HIM! *(to audience)* Can't find any good help these days!

(all run offstage, bumping into each other in their haste)

ACT 2 SCENE 2

(enter OLIVER)

OLIVER: *(to audience)* I'm out running an errand for Mr. Brownlow to prove that I'm a trustworthy boy. I can't keep hanging out with thieves, right?

(enter NANCY, who runs over to OLIVER and grabs him; SIKES, FAGIN, and DODGER enter shortly after and follow NANCY)

NANCY: Oh my dear brother! I've found him! Oh! Oliver! Oliver!

OLIVER: What!?!? I don't have a sister!

NANCY: You do now, kid. Let's go. *(she drags OLIVER to FAGIN)*

FAGIN: Dodger, take Oliver and lock him up.

DODGER: *(to OLIVER)* Sorry, dude. *(DODGER and OLIVER start to exit)*

OLIVER: Aw, man! Seriously? I just found a good home...

NANCY: Don't be too mean to him, Fagin.

OLIVER: *(as he's exiting)* Yeah, don't be too mean to me, Fagin!

SIKES: *(mimicking NANCY)* Don't be mean, Fagin. Wah, wah, wah. Look, I need Oliver to help me rob a house, okay? He is just the size I want to fit through the window. All sneaky ninja like.

The Tempest for Kids

PROSPERO: Hast thou, spirit, performed to point the tempest that I bade thee?

ARIEL: What? Was that English?

PROSPERO: *(Frustrated)* Did you make the storm hit the ship?

ARIEL: Why didn't you say that in the first place? Oh yeah! I rocked that ship! They didn't know what hit them.

PROSPERO: Why, that's my spirit! But are they, Ariel, safe?

ARIEL: Not a hair perished.

PROSPERO: Woo-hoo! All right. We've got more work to do.

ARIEL: Wait a minute. You're still going to free me, right, Master?

PROSPERO: Oh, I see. Is it sooooo terrible working for me? Huh? Remember when I saved you from that witch? Do you? Remember when that blue-eyed hag locked you up and left you for dead? Who saved you? Me, that's who!

ARIEL: I thank thee, master.

PROSPERO: I will free you in two days, okay? Sheesh. Patience is a virtue, or haven't you heard. Right. Where was I? Oh yeah... I need you to disguise yourself like a sea nymph and then... *(PROSPERO whispers something in ARIEL'S ear)* Got it?

ARIEL: Got it. *(ARIEL exits)*

PROSPERO: *(to MIRANDA)* Awake, dear heart, awake!

(MIRANDA yawns loudly)

PROSPERO: Shake it off. Come on. We'll visit Caliban, my slave.

MIRANDA: The witch's son? You mean the MONSTER! He's creepy and stinky!!!

PROSPERO: Mysterious and sneaky,

MIRANDA: Altogether freaky,

MIRANDA & PROSPERO: He's Caliban the slave!!! *(snap, snap!)*

PROSPERO: *(Calls offstage)* What, ho! Slave! Caliban!

(enter CALIBAN)

CALIBAN: Oh, look it's the island stealers! This is my home! My mother, the witch, left it to me and now you treat me like dirt.

MIRANDA: Oh boo-hoo! I used to feel sorry for you, I even taught you our language, but you tried to hurt me so now we have to lock you in that cave.

CALIBAN: I wish I had never learned your language!

PROSPERO: Go get us wood! If you don't, I'll rack thee with old cramps, and fill all thy bones with aches!

CALIBAN: *(to AUDIENCE)* He's so mean to me! But I have to do what he says. ANNOYING! *(exit CALIBAN)*

(enter FERDINAND led by "invisible" ARIEL)

ARIEL: *(Singing)* Who let the dogs out?! Woof, woof, woof!! *(Spookily)* The watchdogs bark; bow-wow, bow-wow!

FERDINAND: *(Dancing across stage)* Where should this music be? Where is it taking me! What's going on?

ABOUT THE AUTHORS

KHARA C. BARNHART first fell in love with Shakespeare in 8th grade after reading Hamlet, and she has been an avid fan ever since. She studied Shakespeare's works in Stratford-upon-Avon, and graduated with a degree in English from UCLA. Khara is lucky to have a terrific career and a charmed life on the Central Coast of CA, but what she cherishes most is time spent with her husband and children. She is delighted to have this chance to help kids foster their own appreciation of Shakespeare in a way that is educational, entertaining, and most importantly, fun!

BRENDAN P. KELSO came to writing modified Shakespeare scripts when he was taking time off from work to be at home with his newly born son. "It just grew from there". Within months, he was being asked to offer classes in various locations and acting organizations along the Central Coast of California. Originally employed as an engineer, Brendan never thought about writing. However, his unique personality, humor, and love for engaging the kids with The Bard has led him to leave the engineering world and pursue writing as a new adventure in life! He has always believed, "the best way to learn is to have fun!" Brendan makes his home on the Central Coast of California and loves to spend time with his wife and son.

CAST AUTOGRAPHS

www.ingramcontent.com/pod-product-compliance
Lightning Source LLC
Chambersburg PA
CBHW051336170526
45166CB00002B/843